A MONTH OF

Wisdom

31 Daily Affirmations Inspired by Proverbs

ELYSHIA J. DAVIS

Lovesculture.com
Copyright © 2024 Elyshia J. Davis
ISBN: 9798987848135
All rights reserved.

Unless otherwise indicated, scripture quotations marked KJV are taken from the King James Version of the Bible.

First printing 2025.

Lord, thank You for Your wisdom, promises and guidance.
Your love, grace and mercy are unfathomable.

Table of Contents

A MONTH OF WISDOM

INTRODUCTION

A Month of Wisdom: 31 Daily Affirmations Inspired by Proverbs" takes readers on an insightful and transformative journey through the wisdom found in the book of Proverbs. Using Proverbs as a source of timeless knowledge, this book provides readers with daily doses of motivation, guidance, and inspiration for a month.

Enjoy reading an affirmation each day that is based on the corresponding Proverbs chapter. These affirmations cover a wide range of topics, including kindness, persistence, wisdom, honesty, and the pursuit of virtue. The purpose of affirmations is to deeply resonate with readers by serving as a powerful reminder of God's unchanging truths and practical guidance for daily living. For the bold and those who are determined to receive the benefits of the Lord, it also serves to speak the Word of God over your life.

Readers are urged to consider each affirmation, reflect on its meaning, declare it over their life, and apply it to their life for the course of the 31-day journey. As readers immerse themselves in the affirmations, I believe they will begin to experience a positive shift in their mindset and attitude. They will gain a deeper understanding of the biblical teachings found in Proverbs and how to apply them to modern-day challenges and opportunities.

The significance of pursuing knowledge and insight as a society and as individuals are emphasized in this book. It serves as a reminder to readers of the profound influence that their decisions, words, and deeds may have on both their own and other people's lives. By embracing these affirmations, readers are encouraged to make positive changes in their behavior and interactions, cultivating a life that aligns with God's divine plan.

A MONTH OF WISDOM

A Month of Wisdom: 31 Daily Affirmations Inspired by Proverbs" is not merely a book to be read and forgotten but a daily guide to spiritual growth and transformation. It empowers readers to develop a strong foundation of faith and wisdom while building character and integrity. As they apply these affirmations into their lives, readers are guided by the wisdom of Proverbs to live a meaningful and purposeful existence.

This book provides a haven for people looking for inner calm, direction, and purpose in this fast-paced world. It is a helpful tool for anybody looking for encouragement, spiritual development, and a life full of God's gifts and wisdom, whether they read it alone or as part of a group study.

DAY 1

I am a life-long student of wisdom and instruction. I learn to understand the words of the wise. From the wise:

- I humbly receive the instruction of wisdom, justice, judgment, and equity.

- I gain understanding, knowledge, and discretion. As a result, I hear and put into action the wisdom that I attain, increasing in my learning from one level to the next.

- I gain wisdom by listening to parables and teachings of the wise.

- I gain understanding by acquiring wise counsel to understand the words of the wise and their mysteries.

The fear of the Lord is the beginning of knowledge; therefore, I attend to His wisdom and instruction. His instructions and teachings are essential for my life.

I answer the call of Wisdom, Who pours into me, and makes her words known unto me. I receive Wisdom's counsel, and I respect her correction. I listen and do what Wisdom tells me; therefore, I dwell safely with Christ, and I am at peace, fearing no evil.

DAY 2

I incline my ear unto Wisdom and apply my heart to understanding. I fervently seek knowledge of the Lord and lift up my voice for understanding of the Gospel. As I seek her as silver, and search for her as for hidden treasures, then I understand the fear of the Lord, and find the knowledge of God. The Lord gives wisdom: out of his mouth, I receive knowledge and understanding. He lays up sound wisdom for me: He is my protection. The Lord guides me in righteousness and on the paths of judgment; His way leads me to everlasting life. Therefore, I understand and walk in righteousness, justice, equity, and every good path.

When wisdom enters my heart, and knowledge is pleasant unto my soul; discretion preserves me, understanding keeps me: to deliver me from the way of the evil man, from the man that speaks perverse things; to deliver me from idolatry and words of seduction about any ungodly thing. That I may walk in the way of good people and keep the paths of the righteous. For the upright shall dwell in the land of the Lord, and those of Christ shall remain in it.

DAY 3

The doctrine of Christ is written in my heart; with it, shall everlasting life and peace be added to me. I abide in the mercy and truth of God. I extend mercy to others and the truth of the Gospel is written upon my heart. I have found favor and good understanding in the sight of God and man. I trust in the Lord with all my heart; and I do not lean unto my own understanding. In all my ways I acknowledge Him, and He directs my paths.

I departed from evil because of my sincere reverence for the Lord; I fear and respect Him. My spiritual health and wellness have increased, I have been strengthened against temptations, and I am encouraged to walk in my purpose to fulfill His will for my life.

The earth is the Lord's, and the fullness thereof; the world, and they that dwell therein (Psalm 24:1). Yet, I honor Him with the wealth and riches He has given me to steward, by giving to Him the first fruits of all my increase and giving charity to those in need. Consequently, the Lord makes provisions for me in abundance so that I am not without.

I welcome the Lord's correction as it aligns my mind and ways with Christ's. The Lord corrects those whom He loves. In Him I find wisdom and receive understanding. The wisdom and understanding that I gain in the correction of the Lord is far better than any riches that can be gained in the world.

Riches of the world cannot be compared to the Wisdom of God. His wisdom leads me to eternal life, wealth of grace, and eternal glory. In wisdom, I received the salvation of Christ, and

A MONTH OF WISDOM

I experience His peace. Wisdom is a tree of life that I will continue to draw from for the sanctity of my life. By this same wisdom, the Lord created earth and by understanding He established the heavens. By His knowledge, the bodies of water were separated and the clouds, which fill with water, and drop down dew to replenish the earth.

I will keep sound wisdom and discretion as they are life unto my soul, and a testament in my life. Wisdom keeps me safe so that I do not stumble. When I lay down to sleep, my sleep is sweet, and I sleep in peace. I am neither afraid of any sudden troubles nor of threats of man. For the Lord is my confidence; He keeps me from the snares of temptation.

I will not withhold good from its rightful recipients, when it is in the power of my hand to give; rather, I will give without delay.

I set my heart to love my neighbor in patience, kindness, mercy, grace, and truth. I speak well of my neighbor, I do right by them and seek ways to bless them as I am a representative of God. Should my neighbor harm me, God will avenge me (Romans 12:19).

I am content with the portion God has for me. He is my focus, and I desire to be more like Him. I venture to please the Lord in how I live. He shares His Word and His secrets with me so that I may thrive. The Lord continually blesses my home. I receive His grace, and I inherit glory from the Lord.

DAY 4

God instructs me, I listen and fulfill His instructions. I seek to know and understand His teaching. He gives me good doctrine that saves and blesses my life. I will not abandon His teachings. My heart will retain His words. Because I keep His commandments, He places a hedge of protection around me and blesses my life.

I meditate on wisdom and understanding. My devotion to wisdom preserves and keeps me. The wisdom of God is far superior to anything; therefore, I acquire wisdom and understanding. I embrace and express wisdom and understanding in every area of my life. In return, wisdom endorses me and brings honor to me. He gives me grace and delivers glory to me.

By receiving His sayings, the years of my life shall be many. The Lord teaches me in the way of wisdom. He leads me in right paths, so that as I walk, I will be preserved and not stumble. I will walk in liberty. The Lord instructs me and teaches me in the way that I should go; He counsels me with His eye (Psalm 32:8). Therefore, I will hold on to His instructions and I will not let them go; His Word is life.

I walk the paths that the Lord leads me on. This path is as the shining light, that shines more and more unto the perfect day of glory. I attend my ears to the Word of God. He is my focus and the center of my life. I keep His Word at the center of my heart. His Word is life to me and health to my soul and body.

I will diligently guard my heart so that it remains right and healthy to operate in the love of God. For out of the heart are the issues of life. Out of my mouth flows words of blessings (i.e., encouragement, love, comfort, grace), and I surround myself with others who are of the same mind. I will not turn to the left or to the right, but I keep my focus on the Lord. My path has been established in Him. My heart is rooted and grounded in His love. I choose His path, and no other will I follow.

DAY 5

I focus my attention on the wisdom of the Lord. I intensely and attentively listen to understand that I may have discretion and use it in how I think, speak, and behave. I will not fall prey to ungodly manipulation or seduction of doctrine. I purposefully and actively renew my mind in the doctrine of Christ. I submit myself to His instruction and correction. I obey Christ and those who teach, reveal, and instruct me in the knowledge and wisdom of God.

I am faithful to the Lord, seeking no other god. I sow His Word to be planted in the heart of man as if it were seeds. My heart is secure in the Lord. My path of life is set. I stubbornly pursue the heart of the Lord, and I receive more of His love. I daily renew my mind with His Word so that I may reflect Him to the world. He satisfies me with His love. I have no desire to seek any other. He is my Beloved.

DAY 6

To secure a friend's debt may cost more than I can foresee; therefore, I will use wisdom and not enter into such contracts. In wisdom, I store up resources for provision in time of need.

I invest the time God has given me to fulfil His plan and purpose for my life, bearing much fruit. I am about my Father's business. The Lord provides an abundance of resources, and I want for nothing.

As a child of God, I speak edification, exhortation, and comfort to people through the leading of Holy Spirit. With a compassionate heart I run to do the will of the Lord. His love fills my heart and overflows. I express His love to those around me by sowing and expressing the love of God. His love strengthens me and equips me to do more.

I remain humble, honest, use my hands to bless others, meditate on His Word, pray without ceasing, speak the truth of Christ, and sow words of encouragement, blessings, and love among others.

God's wisdom is written upon my heart. I greatly value His wisdom as it leads and guides me in life. Even as I sleep, wisdom keeps me and when I awake, wisdom talks with me.

God's commandment enlightens me, and His law corrects me with instructions so that I will know how to live righteously and stay away from sin and temptations.

My heart deeply desires the Lord, and to be a blessing to His people as a witness of Christ. He, only, is my God and I will serve no other. To Him I submit my spirit, soul, and body as He is my Savior and my God. He guides me, provides for me, protects me, and loves me like no other. There is none like Him.

DAY 7

I treasure the wisdom of God, and I continually acquire and meditate on it. He teaches me how to live righteously, honorably, and wisely. I am a student of His wisdom and understanding; they keep me from a life of sin and temptation of ungodly things. Christ is the Light, and I seek Him daily. He came that I might have life, and that I may have it more abundantly (John 10:10). The Lord only means to do me good. He is gentle and will not trick or force me to yield to Him. Yet, because I trust Him, I willingly yield to the leading of the Lord. I will follow Him wherever He leads me. I am secure in knowing that He will never leave me nor forsake me (Hebrews 13:5). He is always with me, always watching me, and always protecting me.

The Lord has captured my heart, and I am eternally grateful that He has chosen me. He prepared the perfect offering to Himself and fulfilled the Covenant Law, so that I could be His. What a great sacrifice and gift He has been to this world. And He sent Holy Spirit, who lives within me, to guide me, teach me, and counsel me in all things. There is no greater expression of love.

Because I have been enlightened by the Lord, I can escape the snares of shame, sin, and temptation, as well as the impact thereof, and live a life pleasing to Him. I also look forward to living eternally with the Lord as one who has lived a submitted life to Him.

Therefore, I adhere to the wisdom of God, and I will not give in to temptation.

DAY 8

Wisdom calls and understanding cries out with a message that saves my life as I heed to her instructions. The wisdom of God guides me daily. Wisdom speaks wise things and reveals right things. I heed the guidance of wisdom as she only proclaims the truth. She speaks righteousness and directs me in the way of God. I possess instruction, knowledge, and wisdom, which are better than silver, gold, jewels, and anything I could desire. In addition to wisdom, prudence dwells with me and I possess discretion. I respect and honor the Lord, and I hate evil, pride, arrogance, the evil way, and the perverted mouth. I receive the Lord's advice, sound wisdom, understanding and power. Through God, I reign and rule decreeing justice, and I judge rightly.

I love the Lord, and I diligently seek Him. I find Him in the secret place. He showers me with His riches, enduring wealth, and righteousness. As I walk with Him, I experience that His fruit and His love are far better than pure gold and choice silver. In Wisdom, I walk in righteousness amid the paths of justice, and I am blessed with wealth, which fills my treasuries.

The Lord created Wisdom before the foundations of heaven and earth. She was beside Him, as a master workman; and she was His delight daily, rejoicing always before Him.

I listen to Wisdom, and I am blessed because I keep Her ways. I listen to Her instruction, and I am wise for it; I do not neglect Her counsel. I am blessed because I listen to Her, watching daily at her gates, waiting at Her doorposts. I find life in Wisdom, and I obtain favor from the Lord.

DAY 9

I have been invited to God's house for a feast. I accepted the invitation, and I now sit at the table to learn from Him. I eat and drink of the spread that He provides me to gain understanding. I honor Him by leaving foolishness in the past. I live, I focus, and I pursue understanding that only comes from Him.

I extend God's invitation to those I come in contact with. I pray for the love of God to overcome and draw the hearts of those who are scornful. I posture my mind and heart to receive correction so that I become wiser, gaining more instruction, knowledge, and understanding. Receiving rebuke is humbling, yet I love and honor those who help me to be better.

I serve the Lord and fulfill His purpose for my life as a witness of His love for people. The wisdom of God provides me understanding in how to navigate in life. He blesses my days on earth, and when the time comes, I will spend eternity with Him.

I listen to Wisdom and make wise decisions so that I enjoy the abundance of life.

DAY 10

I am blessed abundantly with treasures of righteousness. The Lord ensures that I have everything that I need. I manage my work well, and the Lord blesses me with abundance. I plan and gather early so that I am always prepared. The evidence of God's blessings follows me. When people think of me, they remember the blessings of God upon me. I receive the Word of God, and I walk accordingly in it. I will not turn to the left or to the right, but I will keep my focus on the Lord and walk upright.

The words that I speak give life to those who hear and receive. I cover the sins of others with love, grace, and discretion. I can speak wisdom because I seek to understand. I search for knowledge to increase my understanding.

Wealth affords me to buy my wants and needs, as well as offers me a level of security that I can purchase, but the Father provides me security beyond wealth. I work in the natural to provide a livelihood for my family and me. I work in the spiritual to strengthen myself in the Lord and to be one of His ambassadors in the earth. I keep the Lord's instructions to ensure that I remain on the right path.

I consider my words before I speak and use discretion so that my words are not an offense to God. Also, when people hear what I say, my words have value, weight, and credibility. My lips feed many.

The blessing of the Lord continues to make me rich, and He adds no sorrow with it. He grants my desires and prolongs my days. I abide in Christ so that I may secure an eternal covenant with Him. In eternity with Christ, I shall be glad.

The way of the Lord is strength to me. It prepares me for and protects me from things I can see as well as those that I cannot. I know what is acceptable to speak; I speak wisdom and bless others.

I shall never be removed from the love of God. I am anchored in His love.

DAY 11

I deal justly with people and live according to the doctrine of Christ that I profess, which delights the Lord. With a humble heart, I submit to His way. My integrity guides me, and my righteousness directs and keeps me secure in the Lord. When the Lord requires my soul, I shall be delivered out of trouble.

I shall be delivered through the knowledge of the Lord when the adversary attempts to destroy me. When God's people are blessed, both the righteous and the unrighteous in that city are in the state of happiness; when things go well with the righteous, the city rejoices.

I hold my peace when I am around those who wish to despise me to avoid conflict.

I exercise discretion and conceal the secrets of others. I have developed a good reputation and people trust me to keep their secrets in confidence. I have a multitude of counselors who are wise and help me navigate throughout life. There is safety and quick advancement in this.

I exercise wisdom and safeguard myself from agreements to pay for other people's unsettled debt. I am gracious, I secure a reputation of honor, and I retain riches. I am merciful to myself even as I am merciful to others. I sow righteousness, then God rewards me. Living righteously inclines me to live with Christ eternally. The Lord delights in those who live upright. Though I may experience trouble the Lord will deliver me. I desire only good and to be pleasing unto the Lord.

A MONTH OF WISDOM

I am a cheerful giver. I sow into the lives of others and the Lord increases me the more. I am His chosen vessel of distribution in the earth. Both natural and spiritual seeds I sow liberally, and the Lord continues to increase me. I could not possibly out-give the Lord. His deep expression of love for people far exceeds what I can express.

When I give to those who experience scarcity, blessings come upon me. I diligently seek good, and I receive the favor of God. I do not trust in the riches I possess, but I trust in God alone. Because I trust in God, He makes me to flourish as fruit on a tree. The spiritual fruit that I possess is a tree of life to others. I win souls to the Kingdom of God.

DAY 12

I love to receive instructions from the Lord so that I have knowledge of how to live life righteously before Him. I pursue the Lord, and I acquire His favor. I am rooted in His righteousness, and I shall not be moved. I am moral, honorable, and upright to my spouse, who lovingly honors and respects me.

My thoughts have been transformed by the renewing of my mind with the Word of God. In His Word I meditate day and night (Psalm 1:2). Therefore, my thoughts are in right standing with Him. And the words that I speak are bold, courageous, and delivers those who are oppressed and downtrodden. It is because of Christ, who is my solid foundation that I stand despite adversity. I am commended by others for the wisdom that they recognize in me. Yet, I maintain a humble heart as not to think higher of myself than I ought, and I remain authentic to not appear as having more than I do. I diligently cultivate and manage my business, and I receive a great abundance in return.

Because I abide in Christ, I yield righteous fruit, and I escape from the snares of the enemy. It pleases me to do the Lord's work and minister to others with the fruit of my mouth.

I hear and put in action wise counsel from the Lord as well as man. Though others may speak offensively about me, I exercise temperance, and I will not seek revenge. For vengeance is the Lord's (Romans 12:19). I speak truth, exhibiting righteousness and healing others with my words. I am recognized as a credible person with a good reputation because I consistently speak the truth. I have the joy of the

A MONTH OF WISDOM

Lord because I promote peace to others. The Lord protects me from evil. The Lord delights in me because I speak the truth.

I wisely conceal knowledge, and I sit in the seat of power because I am persistent, and I work hard. I speak encouraging words to my neighbor, and it makes their heart glad. Because I am God's child and His truth is my standard, I am more excellent than those who do not know Him. I have precious possessions because of my diligence. I am set on the path of righteousness, which leads to eternal life with God: and in this pathway there is no death.

DAY 13

I listen to my Father's instructions, and I move quickly to implement them. Wisdom from God rests in my heart. As I speak from my heart, the words I speak bring life to me as well as to those who hear me. I carefully choose my words and refrain from gossip, sowing discord, or destructive words. For by my words will my righteousness be seen, and by my words I will be judged (Matthew 12:37).

I diligently fill my soul (i.e., mind, will and emotions) with the knowledge of God. I pursue Him daily so that I may genuinely and abundantly show forth the characteristics of God as a testimony of who He is to others. Love reigns in my heart; I have no appetite for lying. It is my attraction to God's love, grace, and mercy, as well as my desire to have a loving relationship with Him for eternity, which keeps me on His path.

I neither boast about riches that I have nor riches that I do not have (i.e., I do not appear to be rich, yet, broke). I save, I invest, and I am charitable. My wealth allows me protection that may be purchased, but it is the Lord who protects my spirit and soul. Jesus is the Light within me that will never be put out. He rejoices and blesses me with a fulness of joy. With a humble heart I am well advised, and I receive a wealth of wisdom. My wealth is generated by my labor and my acquired wisdom.

Receiving and experiencing the promises of God gives me life and joy. I love, respect, and submit to God's Word and He rewards me. His Word is a fountain of life that keeps me safe naturally and spiritually. People acknowledge my good understanding, and it positions me for favor amongst them. In all that I do, I seek knowledge to increase my understanding. Health and well-being are mine. I humbly welcome and receive correction from others, so that I may notice my shortcomings and choose to become a better me. My consistency and genuine humility in doing this produces honor from others.

I accomplish my desires, and it is sweet to my soul. I am wise because I receive counsel from the Lord, and I surround myself with people who are wiser than me. Good pursues me because of my right standing with God. With wisdom, I diligently structure and protect my wealth to leave a legacy for my children's children. I gradually and with intention build upon a firm foundation to ensure my success and the success of my legacy. I love my children; therefore, I correct them early and I am an example before them of how to live in love, integrity, respect, and honor. The Lord supplies my needs, and it is satisfying to my soul.

DAY 14

God gives me wisdom to build my house and make a loving home for my family. I attend to the needs of my household so that there is no lack.

God's Word is hidden in my heart, and in love I live righteously before Him. The words I speak bear witness of my relationship with God. I speak humbly with discretion. I receive much increase in what I put my hands to because as God leads me, I work in excellence to display His goodness to the world.

I am a faithful witness, and I will not lie. I continuously seek God for spiritual understanding; therefore, knowledge of the Kingdom comes easy to me. I sit in the company of the wise to gain wisdom and to advance on my path of life. I understand my God-given purpose and I will exhaust all means to fulfill it with the greatest impact for others. I receive God's favor because I am faithful to support His vision. His favor is upon every area of my life and as a result, I shall flourish. I am satisfied in the goodness of the Lord.

I consider the words of others, and I determine whether I agree with their reasoning or if their reasoning is contrary to Kingdom standards. I depart from evil. I only implement godly counsel, I display the fruit of the Spirit, and I sit in the seat of those who are humble, meek, and God-fearing. I am blessed to have the knowledge of God written on the tablet of my heart. The evidence of His knowledge is heard in my words and displayed in my actions and behavior.

A MONTH OF WISDOM

My friends and enemies respect me. I stretch my hand out to the poor and have mercy on them. The love of God shed abroad in my heart makes room for everyone. I am a tangible expression of God's love in the earth. I plan and do good towards my neighbor, and they are blessed.

God sets the vision, and I diligently work to accomplish it. In return, I reap the profits of my labor in abundance. The abundance of my riches is the evidence of wisdom implemented. The evidence of wisdom I have easily affords me the influence, respect, and honor of others.

I boldly speak the truth of God's goodness and win souls into the Kingdom of God. My strong confidence comes from God. He is my Refuge. He is my fountain of life, and I have departed from the snares of death. Therefore, I will usher multitudes of people into the Kingdom of God, and the impact, thereof, will penetrate into their 10th generation.

I am slow to anger, and I receive understanding so that I may soberly make great decisions how to progress and gain where I have experienced loss. I extend mercy and forgiveness towards my neighbor. My heart towards others is healthy and light, having naught against any person. I acknowledge and give benevolence to the poor with a willing heart.

Because of God's grace and my alignment with His heart, I believe that I will live with Him in eternity. Wisdom is a treasure in my heart, and though I share it with others, I do not boast of the wisdom I possess. I am just, merciful, and wise as God desires from His people. I will continue to learn His ways and be renewed in my heart and mind so that I may be an extension of Him to those I encounter.

DAY 15

I will give a soft answer to turn away and avoid contentious discussions. I choose my words wisely and with discretion. The words that come from my mouth bring life to those who hear me. They bring love, joy, peace, and more, to encourage others. God's Word is my instruction for life. His Word brings correction to my way of living, of thinking, of behaving. Because I adhere to His Word, I receive His treasures from Heaven. I use the wise counsel that I received of Him, and I disperse it to others so that they may know as well.

The Lord sees everything, hears everything, and knows everything. He delights in my prayers as I live righteously before Him. He leads and guides me. His correction gives me life and purifies my heart. I have a cheerful countenance because my heart is merry. Therefore, I continually feast and I seek God's understanding and knowledge.

I reverentially fear the Lord, and His love dwells in my heart. I am slow to anger, and strife does not have its way with me. The path of the righteous is pleasant as I take on Christ's yoke. For His yoke is easy and His burden is light. My father and mother are blessed, and their hearts are merry as they observe me walking in Wisdom's path and receive Her treasures.

The treasures of Wisdom and Understanding are written on my heart, and I walk uprightly. I seek a multitude of wise counselors in life, as a result my purposes are successfully accomplished. With wisdom I offer solutions to people's problems, and it brings me joy. With Wisdom I advise, counsel, and speak words of comfort to those in distress.

A MONTH OF WISDOM

This Wisdom that I have is a gift given by God. As I walk in His wisdom and on the path that He set for me, I live a way of life that leads to heaven. He establishes my way. His Word purifies my heart. From a pure heart comes forth pleasant words and a charitable deed.

I study to have a ready answer and to give sound information to others. I seek and draw close to the Lord. He hears my prayers and supplications. He instructs me, teaches me, counsels me, and reveals to me His secrets. He favors me with His blessings and the desires of my heart. I rejoice when God reveals His secrets and allows me to see into and receive understanding of His heart. As a vessel of the Lord, I spread His secrets to others, and their hearts rejoice.

I hear and receive constructive reproof from others, and I become much wiser because of it. The reproof of others gives me a greater understanding of life. It helps me to value and honor my life and have greater experiences.

Ultimately, God's wisdom prunes me and reveals to me what is not acceptable of my life as His child. As I humble my heart and mind, I listen to His reproof. I repent and re-align my heart with the heart of God so that I may be righteous before Him. I seek for and live out Wisdom's instructions. I maintain a humble heart before God and He exalts me before others.

DAY 16

I receive the Lord's teaching in my heart, and I speak His will. He searches and tries my heart and finds that it is purified. I trust and commit my works (cares) unto the Lord, and He establishes my thoughts (in peace) to resolution. The Lord made all things for Himself.

I walk in humility. Because of the Lord's mercy and truth, my iniquities have been purged. I honor the Lord and His goodness; therefore, I abstain from evil. My choice to walk in faith, according to the ways of the Lord, pleases Him, and He makes my enemies to be at peace with me.

I rather have gained little righteousness than have gained great revenue in unrighteousness; for the Lord sees it all. When I, as a daughter of God, plan my way, He will direct my path so that despite troubles I may encounter, I will remain safe.

What the Lord decrees concerning my life is set. What He has spoken will surely come to pass. He deals with me according to my deeds. Therefore, I align my heart to His and I live and walk in righteousness. I delight in those who have righteous lips and speak righteously.

My soft answer calms those with a heart of wrath. I am favored and I receive an abundance of blessings from the Lord. This includes wisdom and understanding; worldly goods cannot compare to these.

My desire to live righteously before the Lord, causes me to depart from evil, which saves my soul. I walk in humility as I learn and grow in the Lord; He keeps me steady and surefooted. With a humble heart, I submit to the ways and doctrine of Christ. With humility and trust in the wisdom of the Lord, I am better able to assess matters and have good outcomes.

As a continuing student of the Lord's, I will gain understanding. As one who teaches, the message I communicate will increase my understanding the more. My knowledge and understanding are a well of life. My heart teaches my mouth to speak wise things. I continuously increase my learning in the Word of God. I share the Gospel, which is sweet to the soul, and health to the bones. I constantly seek the Lord's counsel to ensure I am on and remain on the path that leads to eternal life. I laboriously search, study, and apply the Word of God to my life so that my soul may be fulfilled and equipped to address life experiences. Even in old age, I will walk in righteousness before the Lord and teach others His ways. In meekness, I will exhibit self-control and be slow to get angry. Nothing is by happenstance; God is in control of all.

DAY 17

I am filled with the peace of God. The Lord entrusts me to guide and counsel His children. As a result, I shall receive eternal blessings. He loves me; therefore, He examines and tests my heart through afflictions in order to purify me from sin. I carefully attend to and listen to the counsel of the Lord. I honor the poor for they are loved and valued by the Lord. He is glorified when I guide people to Him to receive salvation and teach them His ways. The people are thankful to receive teaching and discipleship that helps them to align with the heart of Jesus.

I speak and I live according to the Gospel of Christ. I align my decisions to His Word. I will not be bribed or convinced to knowingly live outside of His will.

Because I love my neighbor, I cover their transgression even as Christ covers mine. In love, I will remind them of God's standard, yet if they do not receive correction, I will continue to pray for them that God will change their heart. I celebrate those who do good to follow the Lord and uphold His standards. The love of God lives in me; therefore, I have no appetite for contention or strife in my life. I will not validate or justify those who do wicked or those who condemn others who are innocent. These are contrary to the will of God. I will continue to acquire the wisdom of God so that I may have a ready answer for life circumstances.

A friend always loves. I too, love myself and I protect myself from becoming anyone's surety for what they themselves cannot afford. I contend for the things of God. I open my mouth to speak His truth. I meditate on His Word and His goodness. My heart remembers and speaks confidently the goodness of God. He delights in me and graces me with all spiritual blessings in heavenly places in Christ Jesus (Ephesians 1:3). The joy of the Lord is my strength. I remain in the joy of the Lord, which blesses my spirit, soul, and body.

I will neither take or receive a bribe to pervert the way of justice, punish the innocent, nor punish those who fulfill the office they have been designated to fulfill. I will follow the ways of Christ, and the Lord will give me understanding and wisdom to know what to do in times of trouble. I will trust in the Lord to deliver me from the hands of my enemies.

I will use my words sparingly to avoid the habit of speaking idle words. When I speak things of importance, I avoid idle words, it is counted to me as wise, and I am esteemed as one of understanding.

DAY 18

I will continue to learn the Word of God and seek His wisdom.
I delight in learning that I may understand the ways of God and
the dealings of life. Wherever I go, I carry the love of God with
grace and honor. The words of my mouth are as deep waters,
and the wellspring of wisdom as a flowing brook.

I will judge right, and I will offer no respect of persons due to
status or bribes of others. I will mind my own business and stay
out of other people's personal arguments, disputes, and fights.
My mouth will not add to or stir up contention in others'
affairs. My words are for speaking good, not evil. Therefore, I
shall receive blessings for my words sown and not destruction.
My lips are a blessing to my soul. I do not gossip about others'
affairs nor assassinate their character. I am a diligent worker,
and I responsibly manage the resources that God gives me.

The name of Jesus is my protection spiritually, mentally,
socially, physically, and financially. Those who are righteous
call upon Him and are saved. I shall abundantly increase in
wealth and riches, yet Jesus will remain my protection. Despite
God's promotions for me, I will remain humble and honorable.
Without Jesus, His light and love shed abroad in my heart, I
would be lost.

I am patient to completely listen to a matter before I provide an
answer. Not only will I better understand the situation, but I
will also be able to provide the best answer concerning the
matter. I am a resilient and determined spirit who partners with
the Spirit of God. I can do all things through Christ Who
strengthens me (Philippians 4:13).

A MONTH OF WISDOM

My heart feeds on knowledge and my ears remain open to receive from the wise. My God-given gifts grant me access to be in the company of great people.

When someone judges me based on my words or actions, and my response is required, I truthfully account for my activities and words spoken. I seek ways to do away with contention. I forgive and give grace to my brothers and sisters and do not allow contention to be a driving force between us. I do not keep a record of being wronged by them (I Corinthians 13:5b NLT).

I speak good words with grace to others and my conscience is satisfied. I choose to speak life with my words, as a result, I enjoy the fruit of my words. I have joy. I am blessed. I am more than a conqueror (Romans 8:37). I am loved. I am a good spouse. I am a blessing to my spouse, and they obtain favor of the Lord. I am a humble servant, who submissively entreats the Lord with my petitions. I am a friend, and I show myself friendly. I have joy over the meaningful divinely connected friendships who are as to me as my own soul.

DAY 19

I walk in integrity, and I continue to feed my soul knowledge. Knowledge informs me and wisdom steers me away from traps in life. The wisdom of the Lord establishes my way, and my heart is secure in Him. The foundation and root of my love is God. His unconditional love in me extends to others no matter their status: rich or poor.

I speak the truth as one who aligns with the Lord should. Friends will come, friends will go, and some may stay, but the Lord is a friend that will never leave me. I love my soul (i.e., mind, will, and emotions); therefore, I search for and receive wisdom. I prosper and attain good because I keep understanding. My study of God and the keys of life never ceases.

I speak the truth as one who aligns with the Lord should. His joy is resident within me. With self-control I surrender the idea to express anger. It is my glory and my honor to overlook wrongs, forgive others' offense towards me and I do not take thought of revenge. The love and favor of God refreshes, revives, and prospers me.

I bring joy to my Father and to my spouse. I bring love, peace, harmony, affection, and friendship. My Father has set up a great inheritance for me, and He has prepared me to be a prudent, trustworthy spouse.

I work diligently to fulfil my God-given purpose. I feed my soul spiritual food to align myself with the Lord. I abide in Christ so that I may bring forth much fruit. I have compassion and I help those that are without; the Lord sees this as if I have lent to Him.

I welcome the Lord's chastisements so that it may correct anything in me that could potentially impact my relationship with Him. His correction delivers me from living in a state of anger, contention, and wayward living. It keeps me close to Him. Therefore, I will hear and receive His instructions so that I may be wise in the end. Though I have many ideas and plans in my heart, it is the Lord's counsel that will be accomplished.

I express the love of God through my kindness, charity, and generosity. The fear (i.e., respect and honor) of the Lord is within me, which leads me to life, bringing me security and protection from harm. I diligently read, study, and implement the Word of God in my life. I reap the benefits of my obedience to Him. I welcome reproof as I gain understanding, knowledge, and wisdom that brings me closer to Him. I bring joy and a smile to my Father's face as I am a willing vessel that extends His love to others. I do not give place to those who give instruction that would cause me to err from what I know is right or cause me to live outside of the will of the Lord. I respect the Word of God, and I sow it into all that will receive.

DAY 20

It is an honor for me to be peaceable and not enter into strife. I sow, and in due season, I reap a great harvest. I wisely share the wisdom that I have so that others may benefit from it also. My neighbors testify that I am faithful, and I have integrity. My children walk in the same integrity as me and they too are blessed.

The Lord looks at the heart whether there is good or bad. My heart is cleaned with the Word of God (John 15:3). With the shedding of His blood, Christ purified me from sin. The Word of the Lord is my guide. According to the Word, I live righteously and deal justly with my neighbor. I align my heart to His and follow His Word so that I do not compromise and live in sin (hypocrisy).

I am consumed with fulfilling the purpose for which my Creator assigned me. As a result, not only is my family blessed, but the souls of many people that I impart to are blessed. I speak with knowledge, which is more valuable than gold and a multitude of rubies. It is a joy to help people in need, but I will not willfully walk into a snare for someone else.

Everything pleasurable is not good for me; therefore, I will consume the Bread of Heaven so that I may be filled with Life. My Creator gave me purpose and made it known to me. I continuously seek Him to instruct, teach and counsel me on this journey to accomplish my purpose so that when I come before Him, I can say that I have done all that He has asked of me (Psalms 32:8). As long as I remain attentive to Him and His counsel, He reveals to me the best path to accomplish His will.

A MONTH OF WISDOM

I maintain discretion concerning other peoples' affairs. Neither meddling nor dispersing their information is pleasing to God. I honor my Father and He blesses my days on earth. I am a co-heir with Christ. I have received a portion of my inheritance through Him, yet I will receive the fullness thereof in eternity with my Father.

I will not retaliate against my enemies with evil or wickedness; I keep my heart right before the Lord. For vengeance belongs to the Lord (Romans 12:19). He keeps me safe, and I live righteously before the Lord at all times, aligning my thoughts, behavior, and actions to His heart. I am daily guided by Holy Spirit. I cannot succeed in life without Him. I honor the Lord with that which is holy, and He blesses me.

I surround myself with those who have good intentions, and I find reasons to be a blessing to them. My spirit is a candle of the Lord, examining my heart and mind. Nothing can be hidden from Him. Operating in genuine and authentic love, grace, and truth preserves me as a leader and as God's vessel. They win over the affections of people. Whether young or elderly, I am valuable for the Lord's use. I bare Godly fruit and His wisdom is shed abroad in my heart. I remain open to correction as chastisement is necessary for growth and maturity.

DAY 21

My heart is in the hand of the Lord; He directs it wherever He pleases. I surrender my heart to the Lord, and He examines and purifies it for His glory. I live a life of righteousness and justice, which is more pleasing and acceptable to the Lord than offering a sacrifice. Humility and the love of God resides in my heart.

Being diligent, I produce strategic thoughts that bring about great rewards. It is God's favor upon me and my work that yields great treasures. I bless others with the overflow that God has allowed for me to receive. I live right before the Lord, and I have a loving relationship with my Father. I draw away in solitude to spend time with the Lord and get away from the noise of life.

My soul desires love and to be an expression of love to my neighbor. I attend to instruction from the wise and grow in knowledge. I consider the Lord's heart towards His people and the blessings He intends for us in eternity. There is no place that I would rather be than with the Lord.

As God shows mercy upon me, with compassion, I hear the cry of the poor and show them mercy. In secret, I seek out to help the poor, which saves me from His anger. It is my pleasure to do justice so that I am in alignment with God as well as to be in a community where love, virtue, and respect is prevalent. I intentionally live according to the Word of God. I love the Spirit of God and He blesses me with every spiritual blessing in the heavenly realms (Ephesians 1:3). He protects me from the plans of those who wish to do me evil. It is better for me to live in solitude than to be among those who are contentious, quarrelsome, and intentionally ungodly.

I store up natural and spiritual provisions for later use. I follow after righteousness and mercy, and I find life, righteousness, and honor. God gives me wisdom that overcomes the strong and His righteousness that governs and protects my life. I practice temperance to keep my mouth and tongue from speaking evil so that I may preserve my soul from troubles.

With a humble heart I sit at the feet of the Father seeking His will for my life. Seeking what I can do to advance His Kingdom in the earth. The Lord blesses the work of my hands so that I have all sufficiency to be a blessing to myself, my family, and others in need. I will not withhold my hand from giving. With faith, true repentance, and good intentions, my sacrifices will be received by the Lord. I speak the truth that I hear from Him, and He continues to utilize me as His witness to others. God's Word directs my path in life. No one has wisdom, understanding or counsel that could ever overcome the Lord. I am dependent upon the Lord, and I stand with Him where there is safety.

DAY 22

My name shall be known because of the good works that I do with God. This is more valuable than great riches. Likewise, the loving favor with God and people are more preferred than silver and gold. Neither the rich nor the poor is better than the other: the Lord is the Maker of them all. When I detect signs of evil, I abstain from any activity, company, and conduct that would lead me to sin. Instead, I seek the Lord and His protection; there, I find safety.

The Lord rewards my humility with riches, honor, and life. I keep my soul healthy by aligning with God and avoiding the troubles and snares that accompanies those who walk contrary to Him. I receive training in the ways of the Lord so that life's circumstances and situations will not influence me to depart from Him. The Lord has blessed me with great wealth. I am the lender and not the borrower (Deuteronomy 15:6).

I practice righteousness and I reap the Lord's great reward. In my obedience, He guides me to lead His people. I seek whom I may bless with a heart of grace and compassion.

As I remove the scorners from my life, contention leaves as well. The Lord approves of the grace spoken with my lips and rooted in my heart. He has befriended me and welcomes me into His presence. He protects and preserves people of knowledge that His Word may be proclaimed and continue on.

I work diligently to fulfill my God given purpose. I am in communion with the Lord, which keeps my soul from the temptations of the lust of the flesh, the lust of the eye, and pride of life, the cost, of which are more than I am willing to

A MONTH OF WISDOM

pay (1 John 2:16). My heart is bound to the love of Jesus Christ, where I am pruned and receive correction to transform into His disciple in the earth.

My hands bless the poor with riches God has entrusted to me. In obedience and love I bless those whom the Lord instructs for me to give to, and He abundantly blesses me.

With a humble heart, I listen and receive the words of the wise and knowledgeable. It is pleasant to my soul and my life for me to embrace wisdom. As I apply the wisdom imparted to me, I become fit to advise others of wisdom as well. My trust is in the Lord. He makes known to me excellent things in counsels and knowledge that I may know the certainty of the words of truth. With this truth, I am equipped to answer those who inquire and are in search of the Lord.

I bless the poor to bring relief. I stand for unbiased justice and the protection of people. The Lord is aware of my interactions. He likens my gifts to the poor as if I directly blessed Him; in return, He blesses me.

Friendships are influential and impactful; so, I choose to befriend those who are healthy mentally and spiritually to avoid adopting negative habits that would become a snare to my soul.

I exercise healthy boundaries by not interfering in peoples' financial agreements. Following this principle protects me and my family financially, mentally, spiritually, physically, and socially.

I respect and honor those who work hard and I do not encroach upon what is not mine and what I have not earned. I am diligent in business, and I excel in virtue. As a result, the Lord makes room for me to stand before many influential people, which leads to my promotion to fulfil His purpose for my life.

DAY 23

The Lord puts me in rooms with powerful and influential men and women for His glory. When I sit to dine with them, I consider diligently what is before me. I exercise temperance and I do not overindulge in food or drink. I am wise in my choice of words, remembering my purpose for being there. Keeping this focus, I will not partake of their dainties, which will never be able to sustain my satisfaction. My focus in life is not to be rich, but to do the work of my Father. As I utilize the wisdom that He gives me to fulfil His purpose for my life, He will bless me with the resources that I need to be successful. Ultimately, I'm building up heavenly treasures that I will enjoy in eternity.

I seek to understand the heart of those near me to know the nature of the person. "For as he thinketh in his heart, so is he..." Likewise, what is in my heart will be revealed.

I speak wisdom in the ears of those who will regard it. I bless the fatherless and I do them no harm. The Lord loves and watches over them. As their Redeemer, He will vindicate them.

I apply the Lord's instructions and words of knowledge to discipline and condition my heart. I will not withhold from correcting and disciplining my children. Their quality of life is greatly influenced by my ability to lead and guide them. Their very soul requires discipline to align with the heart of the Lord. When their heart is wise and they speak wisely, I will rejoice. For I will see the fruit of my labor.

The world observes my lifestyle and desires to emulate it. For I am a blessed, God-fearing child of God, who is un-wavered by the dictates of the world. I have a lasting reward in my relationship with the Father, even in eternity. This wealth and treasure the world cannot offer me. "So then faith comes by hearing, and hearing by the word of God" (Romans 10:17 KJV). I hear the Word to learn and grow in my faith. And, my heart is guided in the way of the Lord.

Excessive indulgences lead to spiritual poverty. Sufficiency and moderation are key.

The instructions of my parents remain a guide in my life. I am never too old to receive lessons and wisdom from them. I also purchase truth, wisdom, instruction, and understanding through teachers, mentors, workshops, and books. Continuous education is important. My parents rejoice in my righteousness and wisdom. Their observance of my life makes them glad.

I have given my heart to the Lord, and I observe His ways. Temptation to sin is a deep ditch. Once one falls in, it may be hard to escape. You do not notice how deep you have fallen away from the Lord until it is too late. Therefore, I maintain my relationship and fellowship with the Lord, following His instructions, knowledge, and wisdom. I will fulfill His will for my life.

DAY 24

I am satisfied with the Lord's provision for me. I neither envy those who have an evil heart nor who habitually practice evil. Nor do I desire to be within their circles. Their heart studies destructive methods and their mouth speaks of mischievous things. I will protect and guard my heart from them so that my relationship with the Lord may remain healthy and in good standing.

Through wisdom, I began my relationship with the Lord. My heart is deeply rooted in Him. He is a sure foundation. By continuously studying His Word I better understand His character and His ways. By knowledge, I renew my mind and cultivate my soul to align with Him, so that He is pleased with how I conduct my life. He is my strength. The closer I walk with Him, the stronger I become and the more grace I receive. Wise counsel is necessary when I am faced with difficult situations. Therefore, I have many advisors to counsel me for the different areas of my life. The advice from a foolish person I will not accept.

Those who plan to do evil things are called mischievous. Their plans to do evil are sin, and people want nothing to do with them.

In time of adversity, I will stand strong in the Lord knowing that my foundation is strong and sure.

I will deliver or restore the souls of those who have either been void of a relationship with God or who have walked away from the Lord.

A MONTH OF WISDOM

This is my responsibility as I have taken on the cross of Christ to help save the lost souls. An explanation of ignorance is not an acceptable excuse. God knows man's heart and He will judge accordingly.

Like honey, the knowledge of wisdom is good and sweet to my soul. When I find wisdom, I will receive my reward and my expectation will not be in vain. My soul is protected from the adversary who desires to plunder it. Even if I fall seven times, with God, I will rise again. When my enemies fall, I will pray that God will capture their hearts and will raise them up. I will not be glad when they stumble, as they are still precious in the sight of the Lord. He sees my heart, and this would not please Him. I will neither be worried about evil people, nor be jealous of the wicked. Ultimately, God is judge and because I am His, I shall receive the reward of the Lord.

I respect and honor the Lord, and I will not reject Him. I will remain in right standing with Him. I will be fair, and not have respect of persons, in judgement. I will not call right wrong, or wrong right. This is unfair and evil in God's sight. Right is right and wrong is wrong. A good blessing shall come upon me when I practice this. My honesty and my regard to judge rightly is greatly appreciated. It attracts respect and honor from others to me.

I have vision for what I desire to attain. Until my vision comes to fruition, I will gather all the necessities to ensure that I am able to sustain what I desire. At that time, my vision will be established.

I will not busy myself with other people's affairs unless I am obliged. Should I be obliged to give witness concerning others, I will do so in truth. I will not deceive or lead others to believe what is not true. I will only give them the truth that I know concerning the matter. I will not make this an opportunity to avenge myself for former words spoken against me. Vengeance is the Lord's (Romans 12:19).

The Lord has given me purpose. I shall learn and gain wisdom to take what the Lord has placed in me and bring it to fruition. His Word cultivates my heart and gives me direction to ensure that I fulfil my purpose while living according to His standards. He strategically places people in my life who plant good words and strategies that will help advance me in the way that I should go. He blesses me with the resources I need to build. I diligently do the work to ensure that the Lord's purpose for my life comes to pass. As a result of my obedience, many people are blessed. This pleases the Lord, and He blesses me for it.

DAY 25

It is God's glory to conceal a thing, but it is my honor to investigate a matter to understand the truth. God knows the state of my heart even when others do not.

When sin is removed from my heart, I am a better vessel for the Lord's use. Likewise, when I remove the wicked from my life, I am established in righteousness.

I will not presume that I am invited to stand in the presence of VIPs. I am satisfied even if I am not invited within their circle. It is wiser to be invited that to assume my invitation and be asked (or signaled) to leave.

Patience is a virtue, and one that I will adhere to avoid unnecessary disagreements or lawsuits against my neighbor. I cannot foresee the end result, and it may cost more than I originally anticipated. Instead, I will attempt to cordially settle the matter with my neighbor, and I will not divulge their secrets to others. I will make all attempts to avoid any additional mayhem.

The right words, spoken at the right time, are very valuable. I humbly and obediently receive correction from wise advisors who have good intentions towards me.

I am a faithful messenger of the Lord's. He sends me to accomplish His will, and I accomplish and manage all that He planned for me. I do not have to boast of what I am capable of. The gifts, talents, and anointing given to me by my Lord, make room for me. As I serve Him, He exalts me.

A MONTH OF WISDOM

I exercise patience to know when to speak, and I offer reason concerning a matter. I speak with soft language to influence the hardened hearts. Winning over my neighbor is more important than being right and having ruined a relationship.

I have what is sufficient for me. I am not greedy, and I do not hold on to more that I can manage and enjoy.

I do not overstay my welcome at my neighbor's house to avoid being a burden. It also helps to preserve good friendships.

I bear a true witness concerning my neighbor in love, honor, respect, and mercy.

I depend on the Lord. I have confidence in Him in times of trouble and at all times. He is faithful.

I recognize how to comfort a heavy heart. Even if my enemy is hungry, I will show kindness and give them bread to eat. If they are thirsty, I will give them water to drink. Despite what they may have said or done to me in the past, I will show them love and kindness. For the genuine kindness that I show towards my enemy, the Lord will reward me. Also, I will not speak ill of them. I will not succumb to backbiting as this is not a characteristic that the Lord looks for in His children.

My spouse and I are equally yoked and have a healthy, enjoyable, and fruitful marriage fulfilling God's intent for our union. We enjoy one another's presence.

I am appreciative and honored that Holy Spirit shares with me the heart of the Father. It is His joy (and mine as well) to partner together so that I may fulfill His purpose for my life. I will not forsake my stance with the Lord to yield to those who are opposed to His way. Doing such would weaken my testimony to those He has called me to. Great works will I do for the Kingdom of God. It takes a humble heart to serve the needs of others. In my humility, I will serve those I have been called to, and the Lord, He will exalt me. Should I attempt to exalt myself, He would humble me (Matthew 23:12). I maintain self- control to keep order in my life, to establish boundaries with how I interact with others, and to have an overall healthy way of living before the Lord.

DAY 26

I am a child of God and I live the life that I profess, according to His Word. I receive respect and honor from those who observe my life because they witness that my walk with the Lord is true. In Christ, I am protected from undeserved, causeless curses; they shall not come upon me. I am reasonable, obedient, and governed by the Lord. I go wherever He leads me. Relative to daily occurrences, when dealing with a foolish person, I will not succumb to their speech or thought processes that they express. I will remain silent. On the other hand, if they speak in error concerning the Word of God, I will speak to bring correction.

God planted His wisdom inside of me so that I may carry out His important matters. I speak His wisdom in the ears of people as an extension of Him and they listen. Because I speak His Word with His wisdom, I am honored, and He is glorified. The wisdom of the Lord produces safety to the people who hear and take heed to what they have heard.

God's Word teaches me the way of righteousness, and I continue in His way so that I may go from glory to glory. I have the wisdom of the Lord because He gave it to me. I am able to accomplish much in the Kingdom of God because He leads me and extended His power to me. My success is due to the goodness of the Lord.

I am diligent to fulfil the Lord's purpose for my life. I do not make lofty excuses to avoid work. I am focused and I steadily do the work. Like Christ, I can be found doing the work of my Father. I seek the Lord of how I may increase the impact that I make in the lives of others. He gives me witty ideas and provisions that I need so that I may be successful. I humble myself to serve people so that they too will come to know the Lord. It is more important for me, as a vessel of God, to lead people to the Lord versus me boasting of self- importance and doing nothing at all.

I do not interfere with the contentious affairs of others. Meddling in their affairs would unnecessarily include me in avoidable issues. I do nothing through strife or vain glory; but in humility I am charitable in mercy and grace towards my neighbor. I forgive those who choose to do wrong by me or gossip about me as contention breeds strife.

I have discretion and my words are a blessing to people I speak to or about. With my words I speak life to edify, exhort, and comfort others. Discretion, coupled with a good heart, is precious and adds value to my character. With my heart, I speak love to my neighbor, and with my actions I show love to them. When I speak good things, people believe me because my actions consistently align with my words. I actively love my neighbor. I look for ways that I can be a blessing to them; and the Lord blesses me for being a blessing. I speak truth and honesty in love towards my neighbor and it is well regarded by them.

DAY 27

I am thankful and humbled that the Lord allowed me to live today, and I am hopeful that I continue on tomorrow. Others observe and hear of my life's successes, and they commend me for them.

I cultivate temperance over my emotions to control how I respond to others, to have more meaningful discussions, to preserve relationships, and to be an example of Christ. I am content with the success and the possessions that the Lord has blessed me with.

I have friends that openly rebuke me in love and who will not hear or see me do wrong and say nothing. Because they love me, they will correct me despite the emotional wounds that I may experience as a result. And I am watchful of the enemy who flatters with their tongue but means me no good.

I am satisfied with my great wealth, and I enjoy life more because I am empowered to help others as well. I will not deviate from being a blessing to the lives of others; as a child of God, it is my responsibility to bless others.

My heart rejoices because of the sweetness of my friends' sincere counsel. I have quality friends who have proven themselves to be true friends despite my situation or circumstances.

My righteous living is a testimony to what my parents taught me. I love the Lord with all my heart. I kept myself out of trouble. I am blessed financially to be a lender and not a borrower. With discretion, I bless my family and friends. I selected a spouse, with whom I am well pleased, and they honor, love, and respect me. We enjoy spending quality time with one another. I learned that I am sharpened by those I allow to impart their knowledge and wisdom into me and to be careful who I allow to sharpen me.

The Lord will honor me because I wait on Him and faithfully serve Him.

I realize my good and bad qualities when I see the same characteristics in others. In prayer, I seek the Lord to remove the unpleasing characteristics and to purify my heart.

I am satisfied with all that Christ has done for me. I show my genuine appreciation to Him with praise from my heart through my lips. Though some may praise me, pride will not hijack my heart. I will remain humble before the Lord.

I am diligent to personally know the state of my business(es) and finances. I manage my business(es) and finances so that I can best utilize the wealth that God has given me. I am a great steward of my finances. I store up and invest wealth while I am generating it so that when I cease from working, I may continue to live from it. With my profits I also purchase business ventures and land. I have provisions to purchase food and clothing for me and my household as well as to hire help for home maintenance.

DAY 28

Because Christ is my Savior, I am bold as a lion. With understanding and knowledge, I lead people executing justice and judgment for the fulfillment of time the Lord has assigned to me. With my wealth, I bless the poor so that they may have food to eat.

I live according to the commandments of Christ, which aligns me to the heart of God. Holy Spirit lives inside of me and He teaches me all things. I walk in righteousness and the Word of the Lord is written on my heart.

God transfers profits, made by others unjustly, to me so that I may bless the poor.

I am aligned with the Word of the Lord, and He hears my prayers and answers them. The Lord blesses me with wisdom to lead His people. I teach and encourage the righteous to seek and gain a deeper understanding of Him, and He blesses me with a good inheritance.

God dispenses His gifts of wealth and wisdom, both of which I am a recipient. Though I am rich, I do not think of myself as being greater in wisdom over those who are poor. Those who are poor and have wisdom may prove that they are wiser than the rich.

The Lord has assigned me to a people, and they rejoice under my leadership. I confess and turn from my sins so that the Lord will have mercy upon me. I reverently respect, love, and fear the Lord. He is my Savior and I obey His commands.

A MONTH OF WISDOM

I am a great servant to those I lead. I lead those poor in spirit to know my Savior. I seek first the Kingdom of God, and He blesses me with all my needs and desires. I want for nothing, and He prolongs my days on earth.

I seek peace with my neighbor. I choose to actively love them, and I treat them with kindness, respect, and honor. I live righteously before the Lord, and He protects me from those that seek to do me harm.

I am diligent to fulfill the Lord's purpose in my life. He supplies me with everything that I need to be successful. I am faithful to accomplish what He has called me to fulfill. To speak what He directs me to say. To do what He directs me to do. Where He leads me, I will follow. I will be just and merciful to all. As His vessel, I will not have respect of persons, of which does not align with the heart of God.

The Lord's favor is upon me, and He guides me into wealth. Yet despite the wealth that I accumulate, my trust is in the Lord.

I favor those who correct me with love more than those who would say flattering words to hide what they truly think.

I honor and respect my parents.

I put my trust in the Lord. I acknowledge that I cannot be successful in life without Him. He is my success. He is my victory. My wisdom pales to the Lord's and I dare not attempt to trust my way over His. He is my Leader. In Him do I trust.

The Lord desires that I give to the poor. When I give to the poor, it is as if I have given to the Lord. Therefore, it is my pleasure to give to the poor. I lead in righteousness and the people are blessed.

DAY 29

With humility I receive correction about myself, and I make changes so that I may be perfected in Christ. God has given me authority to lead His people. Daily I live in righteousness, so that I will please God and my ears be opened to what He speaks to me. I lead His people with the wisdom He has given me. Because of my obedience His favor is upon me, and the people rejoice. My parents also rejoice in that they have witnessed my success in life, and I have not strayed away from the Lord.

With integrity, I lead God's people by the teaching and expounding of His Word to assist them in their walk with Christ. God's Word prepares and equips us for the cunningness of the enemy so that we may avoid the snares that they enemy has set for us. Rather, we shall defeat the enemy and sing and rejoice in our victory.

With mercy and justice, I consider the cause of the poor. I contemplate how I may sensibly impact and help benefit them. I use wisdom to navigate the hearts of the people to understand how supporting the cause of the poor will help the community to prosper, though some may not be won over by my words. Justice for the poor will go against the plans of others. The Lord will protect me from any of their vices.

With discretion I reserve my thoughts, and I do not tell all that I know. At the right time, I will release what is necessary to whom it is necessary to tell. I surround myself with people who speak truth, I do not entertain lies. Therefore, those who I employ must be truthful and honest representatives.

A MONTH OF WISDOM

With enlightenment from the Lord, leaders, the poor and the evil know that under the leadership of good leaders are fair and just rules. Under corrupt leaders, the poor are taken advantage of and mistreated. I lead with love, mercy, and justice; and the people I lead are blessed.

With discipline I am refined. I cannot always see what needs to change in my heart. I may not like the process of discipline, but I know that I am better after having received it. Pain and correction lend to wisdom. I avoid much trouble because of discipline. When I receive correction and discipline, I learn and become wise in how to behave, react, and respond in life. I have been given a vision that keeps my eyes on the Lord. I shall enter into His rest and live with Him in eternity. I am one of His, therefore, I willingly and humbly receive correction through words so that I may mature and be perfected in Him.

With patience I consider the effect of my words, choices, and actions. I also consider the advice that I received from the wise to make quality, well thought out decisions that lead to my success in my life.

I am the Lord's: spirit, soul, and body. I discipline my body to be servant to my soul, my soul to be servant to my spirit, and my spirit to be servant to the Lord. I delight in the Lord. In Him my love increases to the overflow. I am a conduit of love, which abounds in me and impacts and influences the lives of others. My honor for the Lord upholds me. I partner with Him to fulfill the purpose that He has created me for. I shall not fear. I put my trust in the Lord, and He keeps me safe in the palm of His hand. On that Great Day, I anticipate that I will hear of the Lord to say to me, "Well done, good and faithful servant." Until that day, I will partner with the Lord to witness to the loss so that they too can know Him as their Savior.

DAY 30

Yeshua (Jesus) descended to earth to fulfill the works of the Father and after having completed His assignment, He ascended back to heaven. The Lord is the Creator and He controls the winds. In the beginning of time, He spoke and set the boundaries of the bodies of water. It is He who established all the ends of the earth. His name is Yahweh, and He sent His only begotten Son, Yeshua (Jesus) to be the Savior of the world. He is Holy and He is Lord of all who will receive Him. Every word of the Lord is pure. He is my shield. I dare not add to His words, but I will speak His truth.

Lord, purify my heart. Remove from me vanity and lies. Let not pride reside in my heart to make me think that I am responsible for my success. Help me to maintain a humble heart. One that will genuinely love you, myself, and my neighbor. With a humble heart, let me not think more about myself than I should. I will keep at the forefront of my mind that you are Lord, and I am your child. You are my Teacher, and I am forever Your student. I will continually be led by Your Spirit and not after flesh. I will fulfill the purpose that You have assigned to my life. Even into eternity, You are my God, my Lord, my Savior, my Comforter, my Teacher, my Righteousness, and my Peace. There is no one like You. As I live out Your Word, You cause me to live at a higher standard. One that is righteous, holy, loving, and genuine. Your Word is my standard, and I will follow You for the rest of my days.

My judgment is reserved to measure my ability to meet and live the standards of the Lord, not to judge someone else. I thank the Lord for my parents who taught me the way that I should go. They guided me to the Lord. In Him, is my heart purified and my mind renewed. In Him, is my success. I am nothing without my Lord. He showed His unconditional love towards me through His Son. He pours this same love into my heart that it may overflow into my relationships with others, both rich and poor. I share the love God, and I am a reflection of Him to others. The Lord is my portion; in Him I am satisfied. I honor my parents for they have successfully led me to the Lord.

The Lord is omniscient. Though my actions may be unseen and untraceable to man, the Lord sees all and knows all. There is nothing that I can hide from Him.

The blessings of the Lord are upon me. His favor is evident. Yet, I remember where He has brought me from, and I maintain a humble heart, carrying out the love that He has deposited within me.

Wisdom comes from the Lord. Wisdom teaches me to store up reserves during my season of abundance. Wisdom guides me in where and how I build my home, both literally and figuratively. Our home is a safe place for my family. With wisdom, I surround myself with like-minded people who are determined and will work together to advance the Kingdom of God. With wisdom, I fulfil the work of my God-given purpose, which will bring me in the presence of powerful and highly influential people for the glory of God.

My boldness is strong because of my relationship with God. I know who I am in the Lord. I walk in righteousness, wisdom and integrity and I am well respected amongst my neighbors. I am a child of God and a co-heir with Christ. I have been given "power to tread over serpents, scorpions, and all the power of the enemy, and nothing by any means shall hurt me" (Luke 10:19). I am a carrier of the presence of God. The Godhead lives on the inside of me (Colossians 2:9). I have all of heaven backing me as I abide in Christ.

A MONTH OF WISDOM

I walk in humility before the Lord and my neighbors spreading the love of God. And I will continue to spread His love and tell others of His goodness until the coming of the Lord.

DAY 31

I was virtuously created with wisdom, integrity, strength, confidence, great character, and love. The Creator created me to accomplish great things in the earth. He set the vision and together we accomplish it and positively impact people's lives. My value far exceeds the value of rubies.

The Lord knew that He could count on me to fulfil His purpose for me. He revealed His plans to me, and I seek Him to guide me in every way that I am able to accomplish it. So that on that Day when I stand before Him, I can do so with confidence knowing I have accomplished everything He planned for me while maintaining a heart of love, faith, and righteousness.

I shout from the mountaintops to all that will hear the message that the Lord has given me. I share the love of God and the Gospel of Christ. I live a life of righteousness before His people and behind closed doors as a consistent representative of the Kingdom of God.

The Lord has equipped me with everything that pertains to life and godliness (2 Peter 1:3). Everything that He has purposed for me to do, I have the confidence and the will power to achieve it. I am no stranger to work, and I will complete my assignment and fulfil my purpose.

I read my Holy Bible to receive spiritual food from heaven. Holy Spirit, my Teacher, reveals to me hidden secrets, and it is His pleasure to do so. I learn the ways of the Lord and His expectations from me as His child. I learn how I am to be a follower of Christ and how to take up my cross daily. I learn what I have inherited through the sacrifice, death, burial, and resurrection of Christ Jesus. I daily build on my relationship with the Lord so that I may know Him.

I rise early in the morning to meet with the Lord in prayer. He leads me in what to pray, or for whom to pray, so that I do not pray amiss, but my prayers are targeted. When I pray, the Lord hears me, and because He hears me, I have the petition of what I ask for (1 John 5:15). He speaks to me concerning my life and the lives of others. I pray for them accordingly. As He instructs me, I reveal the Word of the Lord to those He intended it for.

The Lord has placed His message in me for people that are open to hear from Him through me. With the leading of Holy Spirit, I impart His message in their hearts through the ministry He has given me. Whether the people be great or small in number, I will deliver to the message of God with love.

I draw my strength from the Lord. For He is my source. He is my source of knowledge, understanding, and wisdom. He is my power source. All that I am able to do is because I am connected to Him. He leads and guides me in all my ways, and He continues to lead me as I lead His people.

The Lord is my strength. I study the Word of God to show myself approved, and He reveals to me what has been hidden (2 Timothy 2:15). When I go before His people, I am able to give them a clear and true message that edifies their spirit and soul. Helping those who are unaware and unknowledgeable about the Lord and His Kingdom and bringing them into awareness. Teaching the poor in spirit the Gospel of Christ so that they too may receive His salvation and be received of the Father.

I am not afraid of times of troubles and tribulations. Though it may be uncomfortable and inconvenient, as I journey through it, I become stronger, wiser, and more patient. I draw closer to the Lord and He gives me the grace to persevere. Through these experiences, He leads and equips me to pray for, teach, and prepare those He has assigned to me. So that should they experience trouble, they too will be prepared to weather the storm.

I seek the Lord to be clothed in His holiness and His righteousness. I know that I can only be purified through Christ Jesus. Through Him alone am I able to connect with the Father.

I live my life in a way that glorifies God. Those who know me know Him because I am His representative. I stand on His Word, and I am neither afraid nor ashamed of the Gospel of Christ. It is my goal to make God famous to those I communicate with.

I make known to others what Jesus accomplished on our behalf; I generously spread the Word of the Lord. I carry and deliver His Word wherever He sends me. I possess an inner strength and honor that sets me apart from others. Though I experience challenging times for the sake of the Kingdom, in the end, I know that I will rejoice and enter into the Father's rest.

I have humbly sat to learn and glean from the wise. Now, I too speak with knowledge, understanding, and wisdom. I do not think of myself too high or too low to speak with others. I treat everyone with kindness, dignity, respect, and honor.

I manage well the resources, relationships, assignments, gifts, and anointing God has given me. I actively seek how I may fulfill my purpose and please Him. Those whose lives that I impact and influence call me blessed. Because I choose to humble myself to do the work of the Lord, He exalts me (Matthew 23:12).

A MONTH OF WISDOM

I endeavor to live a virtuous life that will be pleasing to the Lord. It is because of Him that I possess good characteristics, such as strength, honor, kindness, righteousness, holiness, humility, and integrity. He refines, purifies, and elevates me. I look forward to the day that I hear the Lord say, "Well done, good and faithful servant; thou hast been faithful over a few things, I will make thee ruler over many things: enter thou into the joy of thy lord" (Matthew 25:23 KJV).

PRAYERS OF THE APOSTLE PAUL

Below is a collection of prayers prayed by the Apostle Paul. These are prayers that I have often prayed over myself. I encourage you to also pray these prayers over you and your loved ones.

I pray to the God of my Lord Jesus Christ, the Father of glory, that You may grant me a spirit of wisdom and revelation of insight into mysteries and secrets in the deep and intimate knowledge of You, by having the eyes of my heart flooded with light, so that I can know and understand the hope to which You have called me, and how rich is Your glorious inheritance in me, and so that I can know and understand what is the immeasurable and unlimited and surpassing greatness of Your power in and for me, a believer of Christ, as demonstrated in the working of Your mighty strength, which You exerted in Christ when You raised Him from the dead and seated Him at Your [own] right hand in the heavenly places, far above all rule and authority and power and dominion and every name that is named, above every title that can be conferred, not only in this age and in this world, but also in the age and the world which are to come. And You have put all things under Your feet and have appointed Him the universal and supreme Head of the church, a headship exercised throughout the church, which is His body, the fullness of Him Who fills all in all. For in that body lives the full measure of Him Who makes everything complete, and Who fills everything everywhere with Himself (Ephesians 1-17-23 AMPC).

Father, I ask that I may be filled with the full, deep, and clear knowledge of Your will in all spiritual wisdom, in comprehensive insight into the ways and purposes of You, and in understanding and discernment of spiritual things – That I may walk, live and conduct myself in a manner worthy of You, fully pleasing to You and desiring to please You in all things, bearing fruit in every good work and steadily growing and increasing in and by the knowledge of You with fuller, deeper, and clearer insight, acquaintance, and recognition. I pray that I may be invigorated and strengthened with all power according to the might of Your glory, to exercise every kind of endurance and patience, perseverance and forbearance, with joy, giving thanks to the You, Father, Who has qualified and made me fit to share the portion which is the inheritance of the saints, Your holy people, in the Light (Colossians 1:9-12 AMPC).

Not in my own strength, for it is You Who is all the while effectually at work in me, energizing and creating in me the power and desire, both to will and to work for Your good pleasure and satisfaction and delight. I do all things without grumbling and faultfinding, complaining against You, and questioning and doubting, that I may show myself to be a blameless and guileless, innocent and uncontaminated, child of God without blemish, faultless, and unrebukable in the midst of a crooked and wicked generation that are spiritually perverted and perverse, among whom I am seen as a bright light, star, or a beacon shining out clearly in the dark world, holding out to it and offering to all men the Word of Life, so that in the day of Christ I may have something of which exultantly to rejoice and glory in that I did not run my race in vain or spend my labor to no purpose (Philippians 2:13-16 AMPC).